Whisper

BY: KIT FOX

Lady Love

Whisper

Whisper

KIT FOX

KIT FOX

...dria Love was an innocent girl who survived
...in 1692. This is the story of the girl who
...a witch, the witch who became a lawyer,
...he lawyer who ensures that wicked men
...for their crimes against women, one way or
...her. In Hollywood 2020, there is no shortage
...those kinds of men, but when Alexandria goes to
...p Whisper Bishop, she finds much more than a
...w case.

Trient Press

TRIENTREPRENEUR

ISSUE 11

SIGNING DAY

AN ANTIETAM JONES MYS[...]

1985
All-City Series

Vindicator
Series

SIGNING

A FOOTBALL NOVEL

Devlin Culliver

"...not only the football fan but also for the mystery [...] you an unexpected twists and turns, and [...] of race, poverty, culture and abandonment."

[...]d face down in a puddle
[...] morning. One of his
[...] into the mysterious
[...] all the answers
[...] will never be told.

[...]nd to the
[...]dult. He

Devlin Culliver

Trient Press®

NOVEMBER AUTHOR TIPS

Social Media Tips for Success.

- Consistently post.
  - *Daily or a minimum 3-5 x/wk*
  - *At about the same time*
- Keep your posts interesting and engaging.
  - *Switch it up*
  - *Include different types of content (video, polls, etc.)*
- Provide value to your audience.
  - *Create your marketing plan according to how your audience uses the site.*
- Be open to different ideas and suggestions.
  - *Give followers and potential customers the option to leave feedback, questions, suggestions or comments.*
- ALWAYS BE AUTHENTIC!

HELPFUL TIPS

RESILIENT SAILING

10 Lessons to Persevere in Life's Stormy Seas

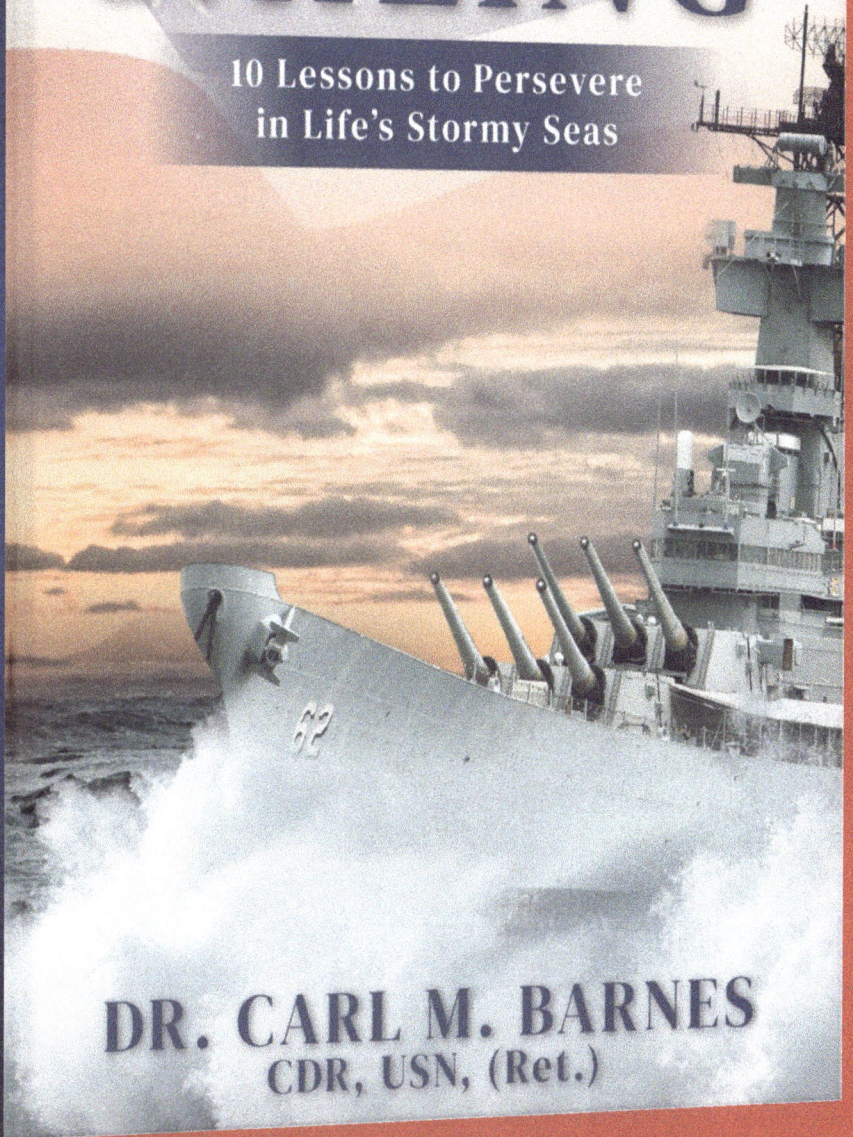

DR. CARL M. BARNES
CDR, USN, (Ret.)

HAVE YOU EVER FELT

Have you ever been abandoned? Have y
Have you ever felt discouraged? Pleas
alone on this journey. Resilient Sai
Persevere Life's Stormy Seas is an emp
healing from your wounds so you can
Land. There is light at the end of YOU
talks about overcoming insurmountab
almost being abort

Based on Dr. Barnes decades of exp
trenches; he has created life lessons v
tools to help you navigate the storm

When you're done reading

◇ Understand what crazy
◇ Develop an attitude of
◇ Face your darkness
◇ Know how to ask for h

Dr. Barnes is th
Effect: How t
Setbacks, 21 D
co-author of
Living. A retire
with 35 years e
(seaman recrui
International
and CEO of CMI

Trient Press®

MENOPAUSE

Women in the Workforce-
(and what they have to say about it.)

Carrot Fertility's Menopause in the Workplace survey shows 79% of women cite working during menopause to be challenging; only 8% report feeling very prepared and informed for their overall menopause experience

MENLO PARK, Calif., Sept. 22, 2022 /PRNewswire/ -- Women in the workforce face significant challenges due to menopause, but they receive minimal support from employers, according to a new Menopause in the Workplace survey from Carrot Fertility. As the leading global fertility healthcare and family-forming benefits provider for employers and health plans, the company commissioned the survey ahead of Menopause Awareness Month to understand the effects of menopause on careers, identify resources available to menopausal women, and bring more awareness to menopause to further destigmatize it in the workplace. An estimated 1.1 billion women worldwide will have experienced menopause by 2025, with millions more going through perimenopause.

NEWS PROVIDED BY: Carrot Fertility

> **WOMEN IN THE WORKFORCE FACE SIGNIFICANT CHALLENGES DUE TO MENOPAUSE, RANK THEIR 50S AS MOST CHALLENGING DECADE AT WORK, YET RECEIVE MINIMAL SUPPORT, NEW SURVEY REVEALS**

Women worry about menopause stigma at work

Of the 1,000 people experiencing perimenopause or menopause across the U.S. who were surveyed, the vast majority of respondents (79%) describe working during menopause as challenging, more than other common life stages, including starting a new job (75% describe as challenging), starting a family (70%), or getting a promotion (62%). Relatedly, when asked what age decade is the most challenging for being in the workplace, respondents ranked their 50s as number one, well ahead of second-ranked 20s.

Most women reported the need to take time off or faced other serious challenges in the workplace during menopause and perimenopause. A majority (54%) have encountered at least one menopause-driven work challenge, including loss of work time and job security concerns. Among the nearly 40% of respondents who took time off due to perimenopause or menopause symptoms, 71% lost more than 40 hours (one full week) of work time, and 30% reported losing more

than a month of work time altogether. Of those who took time off, 59% felt they needed to conceal the reason for the time away.

Other workplace challenges tied to menopause reported by respondents include: perceived losses to credibility in the workplace, worries over job loss due to menopause stigma, and lost work friendships.

""We've made tremendous progress around the ability to understand and address the fertility challenges ..."

"We've made tremendous progress around the ability to understand and address the fertility challenges impacting younger individuals in their work life, but we are woefully behind when it comes to supporting employees with their fertility healthcare needs as they age," said Tammy Sun, Founder and CEO, Carrot Fertility. "The findings of this report spotlight the real challenges menopausal women in the workplace struggle with, including lost productivity and concerns over job security. The survey also validates the need for employers and business leaders to provide age-inclusive fertility benefits for employees."

High employee support for employer-provided age-inclusive fertility benefits.

Most women surveyed were unfamiliar with workplace menopause benefits but highly supportive of the concept. In fact, 82% of respondents see such benefits as valuable. This is on par with the importance of other major employer offerings, such as continuing education.

When asked what type of menopause benefits they deem valuable, a large majority of respondents cited fundamental benefits, such as medical care and support (88%), counseling and therapy (79%), and support groups (69%), as well as other offerings like menopause mentoring (66%), and office menopause rooms to manage their symptoms (58%).

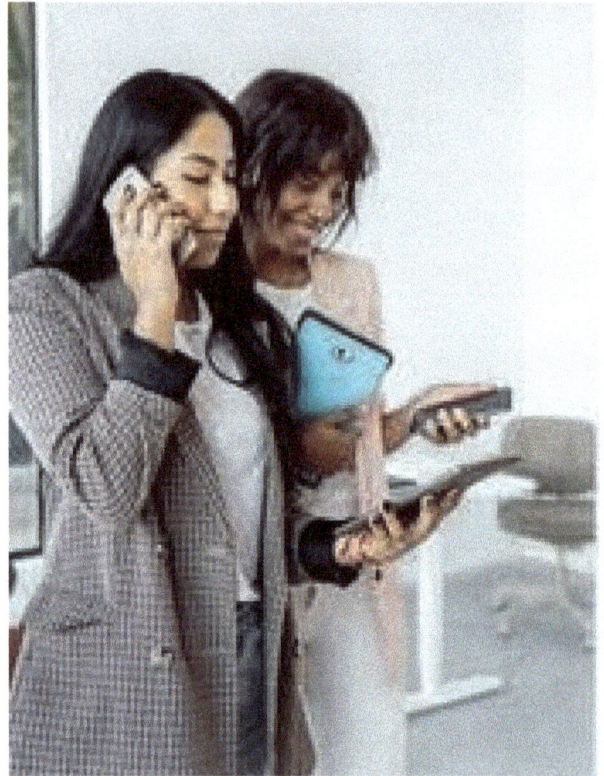

Despite employee support for benefits, employers currently offer few resources.

While there is high support for employer-provided menopause benefits from people experiencing menopause and perimenopause, such offerings are rare and typically limited to flexible scheduling. Only 8% say their employer has offered significant support for menopause, compared to 59% who report no support at all. Among the 21% whose employers have offered significant or minor support, flexible scheduling is the most common (40%).

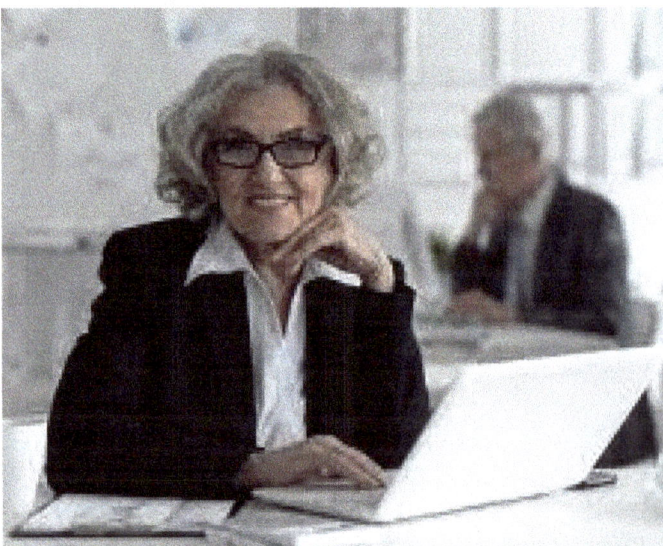

According to the survey, if employers opted to offer menopause benefits, they would gain significant advantages, including employee retention. Of those menopausal women surveyed, 70% have considered at least one major employment-based change due to menopause, including 47% who have considered looking for remote or hybrid work, and nearly 1 in 5 (19%) who considered changing jobs for better menopause support.

Other advantages for employers who offer benefits are increased job satisfaction and productivity. Among the respondents, 92% have at least one reason for believing menopause benefits should be provided by employers, such as employee retention and workplace fairness. Specifically, 62% say it would increase productivity, and 61% say it would improve job satisfaction.

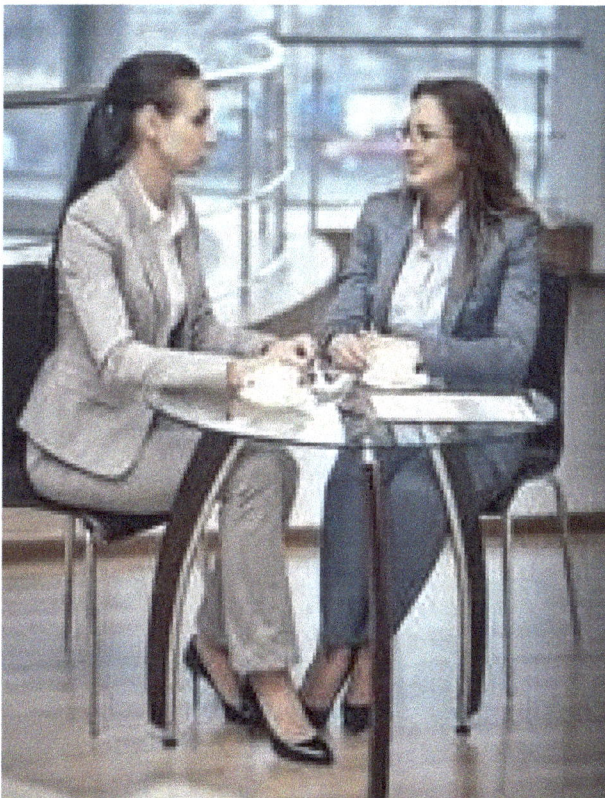

Few respondents feel prepared for menopause: 65% describe their experience as difficult; only 8% report feeling very prepared and informed for the overall experience of menopause; and 47% say they were either not prepared or completely unprepared. Additionally, 59% of respondents shared that they were more prepared for childbirth than for menopause.

Few women feel prepared for menopause.

Despite the lack of preparedness, many women shared that they've experienced both physical and emotional symptoms during menopause. Hot flashes (78%) are the most commonly reported physical symptom, followed closely by trouble sleeping (77%), fatigue (75%), night sweats (74%), and weight gain or slower metabolism (71%). Mood changes (68%) and anxiety (62%) are the most commonly reported emotional and mental health symptoms.

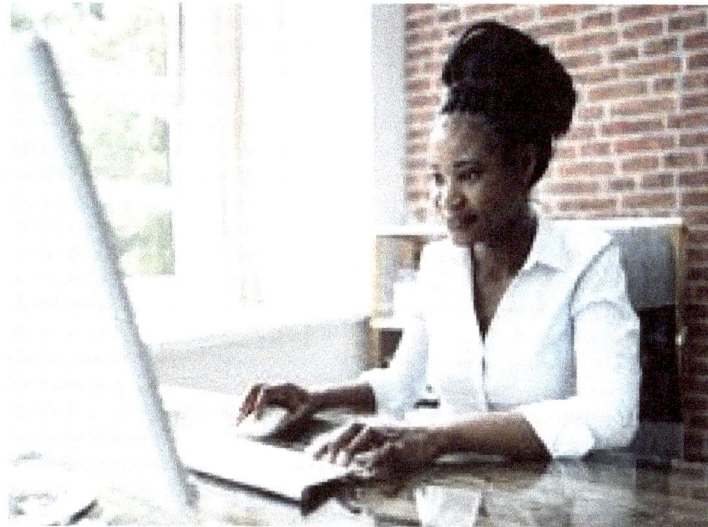

Discussing menopause at work is perceived as taboo; also affects personal and professional relationships.

Additional findings of Carrot's Menopause in the Workplace survey spotlight the perception that discussing menopause at work is taboo, and the significant impact menopause has on respondents' personal and professional relationships.

The majority of people surveyed shared that they're uncomfortable discussing menopause at work: 77% of respondents noted feeling uncomfortable talking with executives about menopause, 63% feel uncomfortable talking with human resources, and 58% with their immediate supervisor.

Most respondents (91%) have sought support for menopause from at least one major source, among which the most commonly reported is a doctor/physician (56%), followed by online searches and other forums (50%). Only 28% of respondents noted turning to their partner or spouse for support.

Seventy-three percent say menopause has negatively impacted at least one category of interpersonal relationships, with romantic life being the most common (58%) and work-life relationships negatively impacted for 30% of respondents.

"The dramatic hormonal changes stemming from menopause can result in symptoms that negatively impact people physically, mentally, and emotionally, in both their personal and professional lives, as confirmed by this survey," said Dr. Asima Ahmad, MD, MPH, Co-founder and Chief Medical Officer, Carrot Fertility. "What's also crystal clear from this survey is the diversity of support and benefits women in the workplace deem critical to their productivity, ranging from medical care to counseling and emotional support groups. We hope employers are taking note."

Earlier this year, Carrot pioneered a new line of clinically-validated, age-inclusive fertility benefits for employees going through every stage of menopause and low testosterone. Carrot customers now have the option to add comprehensive support for menopause and low testosterone as part of their fertility benefits package. For Carrot members, that means they have improved access to providers through a specialized network, clinically supervised education, intimate group support, and more. Members can opt into a personalized Carrot Plan, receive telehealth access to specialized experts, participate in expert-led group sessions, access Carrot-vetted providers that support menopause and low testosterone, and access additional resources.

About Carrot Fertility

Carrot Fertility is the leading global fertility healthcare and family-formin benefits provider for employers and health plans. Companies use Carrot t customize an inclusive fertility benefit that provides employees financial, medical, and emotional support as they pursue parenthood and fertility c reducing healthcare costs and resulting in better clinical outcomes. Carro clinically managed program includes fertility preservation like egg and sp freezing, IVF, donor and gestational carrier services, adoption, pregnanc menopause, and low testosterone support; Carrot Rx®, a premium pharm experience at significant savings; and the Carrot Card®, a flexible pre-fun card employees can use to pay for their care. Learn more at www.carrotfertility.com.

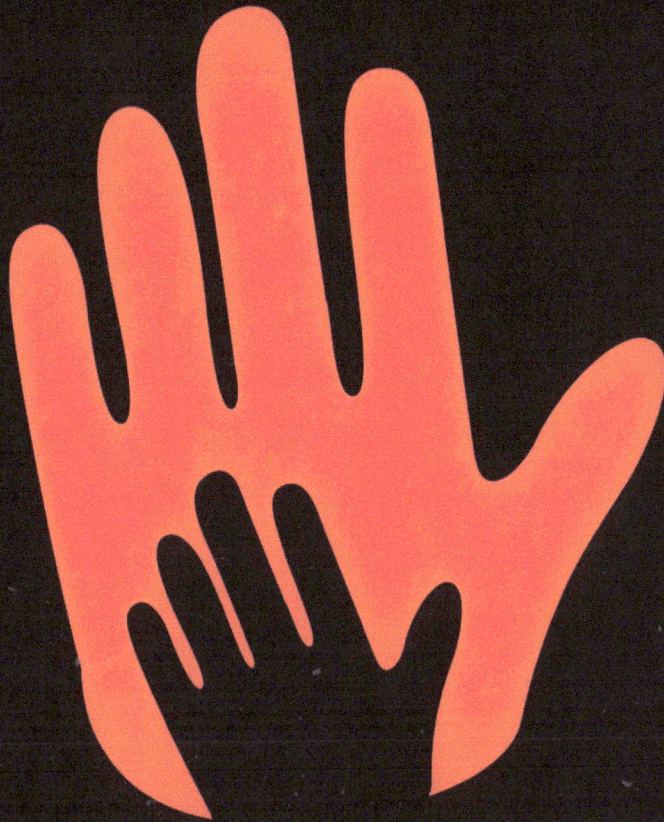

MAKE IT STOP

END HUMAN TRAFFICKING

People are not for sale. Help us stop this terrible happening today.

LEARN ABOUT WHAT YOU CAN DO
HTTPS://STOP-HUMANTRAFFICKING.COM

Joyeux Noël

Why You Need To Promote To The Christmas Market

If you're thinking of making some money this holiday season now is the time to be taking action. More and more people are looking online for their holiday season purchases and gift ideas so it makes good business sense to position yourself in front of them. So today I am going to discuss three key reasons why folks can't help themselves when it comes to spending money at Christmas.

Christmas is the peak spending season of the year. Can you think of any other time of the year when people spend more money? Shops where people happily take their time making their buying decisions are now jammed to the rafters with impatient shoppers desperate to spend their money. Cash tills normally ticking over steadily are almost exploding with people's money and credit card receipts. So what are the psychological triggers for this wild spending spree?

Primarily it's the impending deadline to buy in time for Christmas. People like to be organised and not leave everything to the last minute. There's also the possibility of shops and online stores running out of stock so concerned shoppers are motivated to buy and avoid this scenario. Perceived scarcity is often a huge psychological factor behind a buying decision. Away from the holiday season scarcity provokes people into buying stuff they don't even have a need for!

Another huge influence in buying behaviour at Christmas is people have a lot more time on their hands. Some people don't know what to do with themselves and end up buying stuff online purely out of boredom. It's easier now more than ever to spend money online as it gradually becomes the accepted place to shop. Where else can you buy a range of products that are being offered on top sites like ebay.com and amazon.com at such ridiculously low prices?

Christmas is the busiest time of the year and more and more people are looking to buy their gifts and Christmas essentials online. It's quick, it's easy and they can do it from the comfort of their own home. It's also a lot less stressful for people than having to fight their way around a store heaving with people. As an internet marketer and entrepreneur it's crucial for your success to tap into this lucrative holiday season market.

o find out the smartest ways to position yourself online in front of hordes of hungry buyers this Christmas then check out Trient's brand new guide 'Christmas Internet Marketing' for Free- or nearly free marketing ideas and links.

Free and Almost-Free Promotion

Many books, tapes, videos, and audio files have been created that list hundreds and thousands of ways, sites, and methods for promoting products during the Christmas season, as well as year-round. But you don't have hundreds of hours or hundreds of dollars to spend. You know what you want to promote and you just want to know how to do it for free. To get you started, here's a top 19 list of free methods that you can use to promote your Christmas products this holiday season.

- Sign up for a free affiliate account at Amazon.com. Use this link: https://affiliate-program.amazon.com/ and then select the products that you want to sell. Follow their instructions to get the code to promote your selected products.
- Sign-up for a free account at Sales Spider to advertise your products. Use this link: www.salespider.com/classifieds_post_ad.php
- Register for a free account at US Free Ads to advertise your products. Use this link: www.usfreeads.com
- Advertise your products on Craig's List. Use this link: www.craigslist.com
- Sign up for a free blog at WordPress to promote your product. Use this link: www.WordPress.com
- Sign-up for a free blog at Blogger that will allow you to advertise your product using affiliate links to your product. Use this link to set up your free Blogger blog: www.blogger.com
- Open an account at Hubpages. Use this link: www.hubpages.com
- Open an account on Facebook. Use this link: www.Facebook.com
- Create or outsource 20 articles based on the top 20 toys that you Christmas Internet Marketing - 17 - want to target using your affiliate code. In your resource box, include a link to your free site or blog that is promoting your affiliate product or a product that you have created. Then submit the articles to free article directories.
- Create a new account at Squidoo to promote your products. Use this link: www.squidoo.com
- Create a new account at Weebly. Use this link: www.weebly.com
- Open up an account at PayPal. You'll need a PayPal account to receive your affiliate payments, and also to advertise for free in the PayPal marketplace. Use this link: www.PayPal.com
- Create an account at Google maps. Fill in all the information, and include the name of your business and where you are selling your products. Use this link: https://www.google.com/accounts/NewAccount?service=loc al
- Create a free website through Google. Use this link: http://www.google.com/sites/help/intl/en/overview.html
- Open an online e-zine ads advertising account to promote your Christmas products. Use this link: http://www.mywizardads.com/
- Open an account at GoArticles. Then write five articles with links to your free sites that advertise your products. Use this link: www.goarticles.com
- Open an account at eBay and then list your products for sale through their classified ads section. Use this link for more information, noting that it will cost you $10 for 30 days of advertising: http://pages.ebay.com/help/sell/classified.html
- Go to Fiverr and find someone who will promote your products for five dollars. Use this link: www.fiverr.com
- Using Google, Yahoo, or Bing, search for forums that deal specifically with the products that you want to sell during the Christmas holidays. Then join between one and three forums. Add your signature to your profile and include a link to your free site that sends visitors to the Christmas products that you have chosen to sell.

New Releases

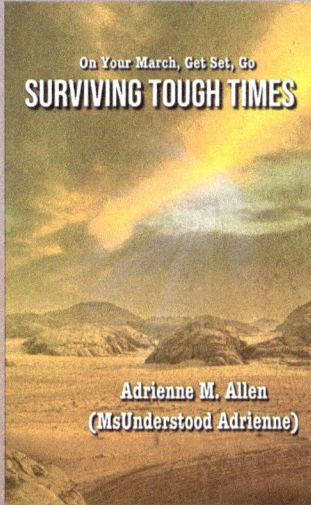

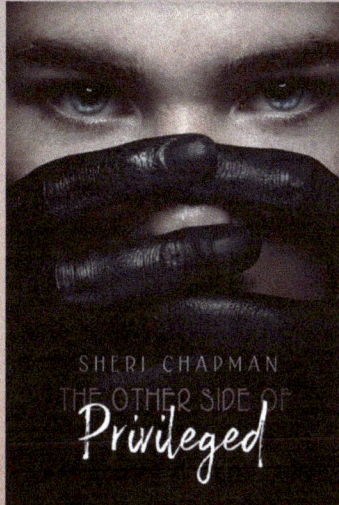

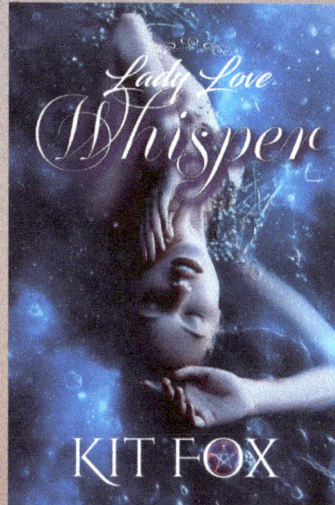

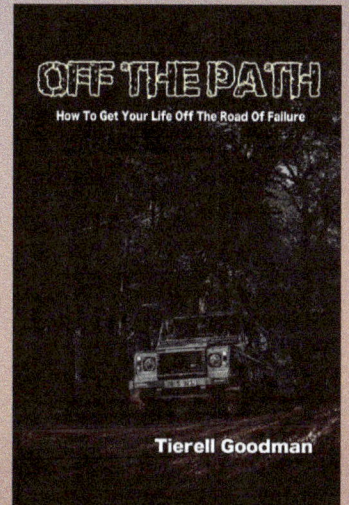

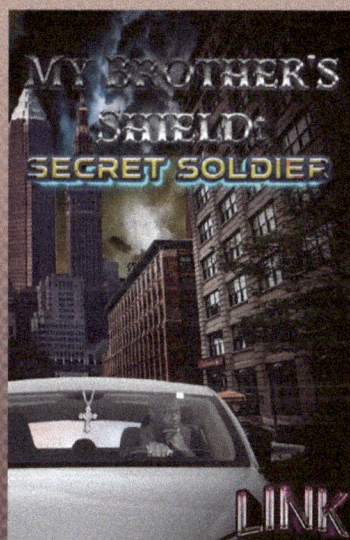

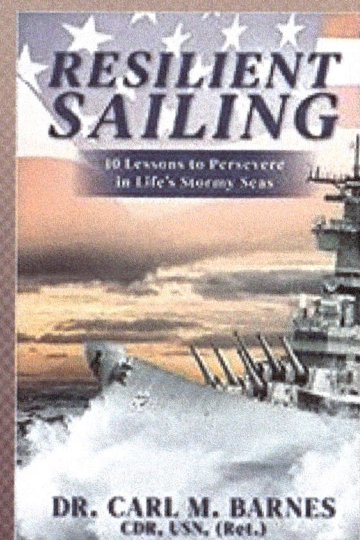

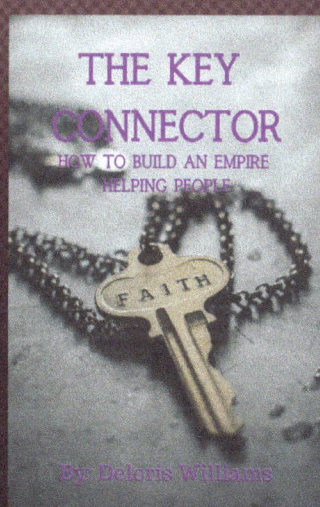

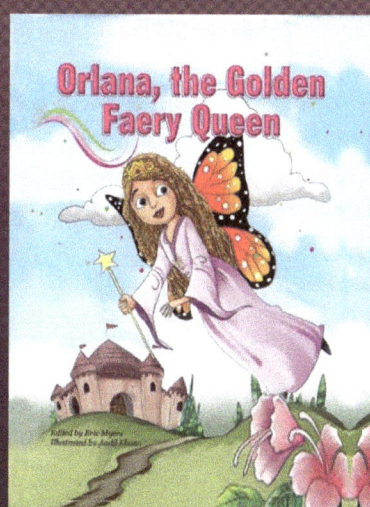

STOCKCHARTS ANNOUNCES THE RETURN OF CHARTCON, AN ONLINE INVESTING AND TECHNICAL ANALYSIS CONFERENCE

The technical analysis and financial charting platform's landmark event returns following the 2020 cancellation of the biennial conference

REDMOND, Wash., Sept. 22, 2022 /PRNewswire/ -- StockCharts, the web's leading technical analysis and financial charting platform for online investors, today announced the return of its biennial investing and technical analysis conference, ChartCon, which will be live streamed October 7 and October 8, 2022. This will be the company's sixth ChartCon conference (the 2020 event was canceled due to the pandemic). Following the success of the first "virtual" conference in 2016, ChartCon 2022 will be the third event to be broadcast live online.

For this multi-day conference, StockCharts has assembled an impressive lineup of industry-leading technical analysts, financial professionals, authors, and educators. Each will have a platform so they can share their expertise and insights with attendees. Over the span of two days, attendees will have the opportunity to join live trading rooms, fireside chats, sector deep-dives, and panel discussions led by these leading market authorities.

"At its heart, StockCharts has always been a platform aimed to build community and create global connections," said David Keller, chief market strategist at StockCharts. "ChartCon 2022 invites investors and top market strategists from around the world to come together and engage in lively discussions that highlight key themes and trends to watch for the remainder of the year."

The list of featured speakers at ChartCon 2022 includes Larry Williams, Linda Raschke, Erin Swenlin, Dave Landry, Martin Pring, Gatis Roze, Jon Markman, Ralph Acampora, Marc Chaikin, Julius de Kempenaer, Joe Rabil, Greg Schnell, Bruce Fraser, Mish Schneider, Mary Ellen McGonagle, Jay Woods, Leslie Jouflas, Tom Bowley, Jeff deGraaf, and Tony Dwyer.

"I am thrilled to partner with StockCharts and join ChartCon 2022 as a keynote speaker to help attendees make more informed decisions about their investments," said legendary trader and educator Larry Williams. "This rare opportunity will bring together market experts from all over the world, and I am honored to have the opportunity to help attendees enhance their trading journeys."

As part of their ongoing effort to bring high-quality, chart-based market analysis to investors, StockCharts is also excited to announce the new capabilities that will be available on StockCharts TV, made possible by the brand new studio opening in Redmond, WA. The new studio will enhance the on-screen experience and improve audio and visual capabilities for viewers.

TO PARTICIPATE IN CHARTCON 2022, VIEWERS AROUND THE WORLD CAN REGISTER OR LEARN MORE INFORMATION AT STOCKCHARTS.COM/CHARTCON.

About StockCharts
StockCharts.com is the web's leading technical analysis and financial charting platform for online retail investors. Founded in 1999 Microsoft developer Chip Anderson, the company has been an industry leader in the financial technology space for nearly two decades, p innovative, award-winning charting and analysis tools to a global audience.
By using technology to help investors visualize financial data, StockCharts.com allows users to better analyze the markets, monitor and their portfolios, find promising new stocks and funds to buy, and ultimately make smart, well-timed investment decisions. With over 1. active monthly users and counting around the world, the company serves an ever-growing, ever-changing array of active traders and inves

MARS WRIGLEY ADVANCES COCOA
SUSTAINABILITY WITH PROGRESS ON WOMEN'S EMPOWERMENT AND PROTECTING FORESTS

BY:MARS WRIGLEY

Andrew Clarke, Mars Wrigley Global President: "Too many cocoa farmers continue to face a series of challenges from poverty to child labor and deforestation. The impacts of climate change and global crises are exacerbating existing vulnerabilities across cocoa farming communities and beyond. This is why we aim to accelerate the transformation of the cocoa supply chain so that it benefits both people and the planet. To get there, we're working to protect children, preserve forests, and improve farmer incomes. We are challenging ourselves and the entire sector to evolve and adopt approaches that deliver greater impact where it matters most – in cocoa farming communities across Latin America, West Africa, and Southeast Asia."

- Mars releases Cocoa for Generations report detailing its latest progress toward creating a modern, inclusive, and sustainable supply chain.

- Advancements include significant progress on its Women for Change program with CARE and key deforestation-free milestones.

- The iconic treats and snacks company has sourced 61% of cocoa through its Responsible Cocoa program, on track to reach its goal of 100% by 2025.

CHICAGO, Sept. 22, 2022 /PRNewswire/ -- Mars Wrigley, a maker of chocolate for more than 100 years, today published its Cocoa for Generations progress report. The report details the company's advancement toward creating a modern, inclusive, and sustainable cocoa supply chain, and 100% of its cocoa being responsibly sourced and traceable from farm to first point of purchase by 2025.

" **We are working to transform the cocoa ecosystem, and while we've made important progress to-date, we're not done yet.**

Amber Johnson, Vice-President Mars Wrigley Cocoa: "We can't do this work alone. The shifts and the scale to reach sustained, demonstrable improvements for cocoa farming families and their communities requires thinking and collaborating in new ways. We are working to transform the cocoa ecosystem, and while we've made important progress to-date, we're not done yet. Through our programs and in collaboration with key global partners, including industry peers, governments, development agencies, research institutions and civil society organizations, we're sharing what works and what we learn along the way. We remain constructively discontent – relentless in our work to create a modern, inclusive, and sustainable cocoa supply chain. One where the environment is protected, human rights are respected, and everyone has the opportunity to thrive."

The report details Mars Wrigley's significant progress in 2021 and highlights notable achievements to date. Enabled by its Cocoa for Generations strategy, Mars Wrigley is strongly committed to accelerating the transformation of the cocoa supply chain. Mars Wrigley is backing its commitment with action.

> *Mars Wrigley's progress against the goals laid out in the Cocoa for Generations strategy include two notable milestones.*

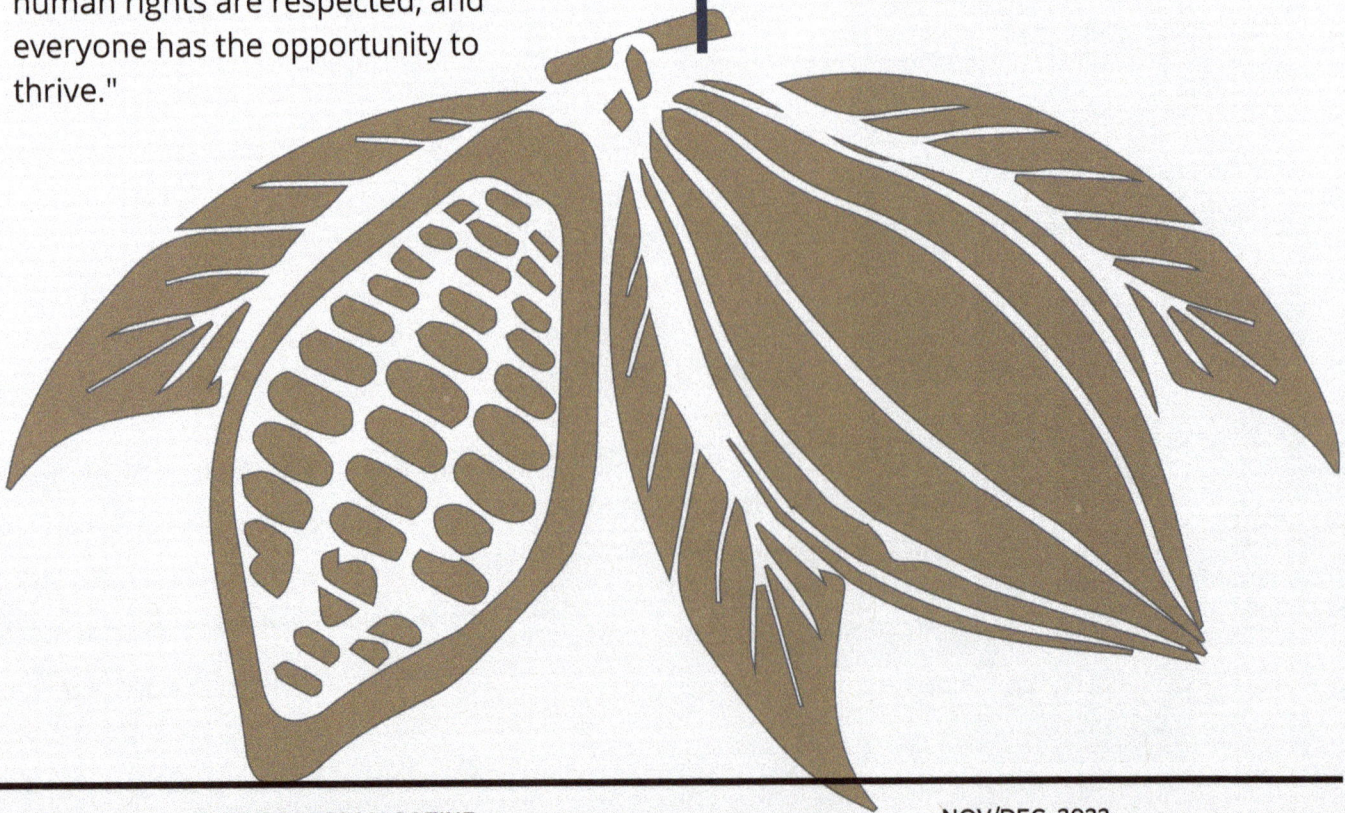

Recently, the company launched two groundbreaking programs that aim to support 14,000 smallholder farmers in Côte d'Ivoire and Indonesia on a path to a sustainable living income by 2030.

- Unlocking opportunities for women. In collaboration with CARE, the Women for Change program has reached more than 77,000 members in cocoa farming communities in Côte d'Ivoire and Ghana, through its Village Savings and Loans Association program. This effort has supported almost 58,000 women, resulting in over $7.4 million in collective savings and over $3.7 million in loans distributed. These funds have been used in a variety of ways, including cocoa farming activities; household related expenses, such as access to education, health needs, and nutritious food; and additional income-generating activities, including growing other crops like rice, and raising sheep, pigs, and other livestock.

- Unlocking opportunities for women. In collaboration with CARE, the Women for Change program has reached more than 77,000 members in cocoa farming communities in Côte d'Ivoire and Ghana, through its Village Savings and Loans Association program. This effort has supported almost 58,000 women, resulting in over $7.4 million in collective savings and over $3.7 million in loans distributed. These funds have been used in a variety of ways, including cocoa farming activities; household related expenses, such as access to education, health needs, and nutritious food; and additional income-generating activities, including growing other crops like rice, and raising sheep, pigs, and other livestock.

"

Mars Wrigley's progress against the goals laid out in the *Cocoa for Generations* strategy include two notable milestones.

- Tackling deforestation. Mars Wrigley is on its way to achieving a deforestation- and conversion-free supply chain for 100% of the cocoa it sources by 2025.
  - One effort driving the company's progress is farm plot polygon mapping, which traces the perimeter of a farm rather than only one GPS point and results in increased traceability from the farm to the first point of purchase; by the end of 2021, almost 80% of cocoa plots from which Mars Wrigley sources have been mapped.
  - Through its suppliers, Mars Wrigley has distributed more than 1.9 million new non-cocoa trees in 2021, helping to increase shade and biodiversity and capture carbon.
  - Achieving its goal of the cocoa it sources being 100% deforestation- and conversion-free will deliver an estimated 20% reduction in Mars Wrigley's total greenhouse gas footprint, progress towards Mars, Incorporated broader ambition of achieving a 27% reduction of value chain emissions by 2025 as well as net zero emissions across the full value chain by 2050.

To learn more about Mars Wrigley's commitments to advancing respect for human rights, creating climate-smart solutions and providing opportunities to thrive under its holistic and human-centric Cocoa for Generations strategy, visit www.mars.com.

About Mars, Incorporated
For more than a century, Mars, Incorporated has been driven by the belief that the world we want tomorrow starts with how we do business today. This common purpose unites our 140,000+ Associates. It is at the center of who we are as a global, family-owned business, and it fuels how we are transforming, innovating, and evolving to make a positive impact on the world.

Every year, our diverse and expanding portfolio of quality confectionery, food, and pet care products and services delight millions of people and supports millions of pets. With almost $45 billion in annual sales, we produce some of th world's best-loved brands including Ben's Original™, CESAR®, Cocoavia®, DOVE®, EXTRA®, KIND®, M&M's®, SNICKERS®, PEDIGREE®, ROYAL CANIN®, and WHISKAS®. We are creating a better world for pets through nutrition, breakthrough programs in diagnostics, wearable health monitoring, DNA testin pet welfare and comprehensive veterinary care with AniCura, BANFIELD™, BLUEPEARL™, Linnaeus and VCA™.

We know we can only be truly successful if our partners and the communities in which we oper prosper. The Mars Five Principles – Quality, Responsibility, Mutuality, Efficiency and Freedom – in our Associates to act every day to help create a better world tomorrow in which the planet, its people and pets can thrive.

FOR MORE INFORMATION ABOUT MARS, PLEASE VISIT WWW.MARS.COM.
JOIN US ON FACEBOOK, TWITTER, INSTAGRAM, LINKEDIN AND YOUTUBE.

preneur
Authors & Entrepreneurs
$10.99

Trientrepreneur
ent Press Publication for Authors & Entrepreneurs
$10.99
ue 4 | July 2021

ATURED
er Special Agent,
Author Link

ARTICLES
ur Time Management
Tactics for Busy
ntrepreneurs

lism Can Help
and Strengthen
the Mind

TIPS
Must have information
for both authors and
entrepreneurs

trepreneur
cation for Authors & Entrepreneurs
$10.99

TRIENTREPRENEUR
MAGAZINE
WHAT'S IN YOUR TOOL BOX

Step into the Spotlight:
Ramp Up Your Business

Lessons from Speech and Charisma Coach Mary Gardner

Lights! Camera! ACTION!

Just a few years ago, those words were used for a select few. People in film and movies. TV anchors and Talk Show Hosts; and families shooting footage on important holidays!

Fast forward to today and beyond, and every person, everywhere, has the ability to step into the spotlight before millions, no matter if they are in their home basement, at the beach or at the office. Your camera is always on your person, and you, along with your creativity and brand, are the Stars!

So how does an entrepreneur take advantage of this new exciting time where we can all have access to our very specific potential client, 24/7, 7 days a week?

The stats are clear! 88% of people say that they've been convinced to buy a product or service by watching a brand's video. 78% of people say they've been convinced to buy or download a piece of software or app by watching a video. Furthermore, Over 40% of global shoppers surveyed say they have purchased products they discovered on YouTube.

While these are exciting times, there is also a problem! There are so many individuals, about half of the population who don't gravitate towards the spotlight, they would rather be in the audience than on stage, and they don't desire to see their name in lights.

But they do want to sell their product or their services. So, how does the high achiever, the introvert and the intelligent entrepreneur become comfortable with the new landscape of marketing, and how do they take advantage of this trend?

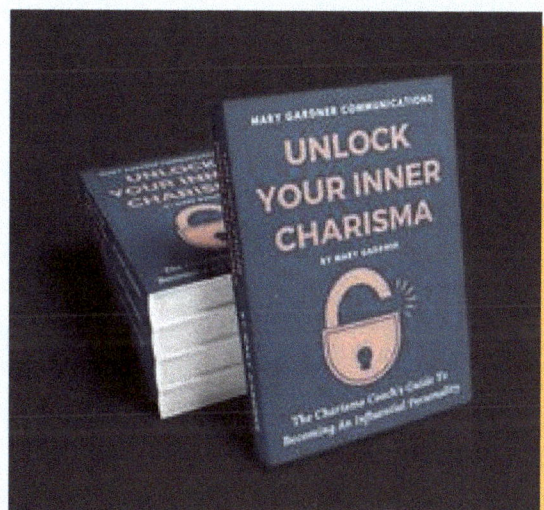

They first must realize that they've learned MANY new competencies as they've grown their businesses so being a rainmaker, a thought leader or an influencer is just one new skill to achieve. Also, if they DON'T find a way to use video and create a personal brand online, that it can dramatically impact sales. It won't allow many potential customers to understand who they are and what they will get out of using their company's products or services; and finally, they might fall behind the competition who has been able to step out from behind the scenes and comfortably into the limelight!

As a long time Communications Consultant and Coach, I have had the pleasure of working with literally thousands of clients through the years to become engaging, likeable, charismatic and graceful at speaking on stage or on video. There is nothing I like better than seeing a less than polished individual, introvert, or a shy individual shed the fear, and blossom into a comfortable and charismatic version of their former self. The transformation feels great to the speaker and they finally access a whole new side of themselves!

In order to let their inner light shine without fear:

1. Be coachable – you didn't get to where you are completely on your own and to get to that next level, being open to getting professional help through individual coaching, or trainings like our Speaker Bootcamps and TEDx Bootcamps, and having support team is a great step.

2. Consider going shopping! Whether you're only appearing on zoom from the waist up or if you're going to be on stage, the saying "the clothes make the man" (or woman) and you feeling fantastic is a quick way to give yourself immediate confidence. So in addition to updating your attire, keep your hair up to date and consider accessories like bold and interesting eyewear and interesting looks to keep people engaged while on video and on stage.

3. On video, keep your desk area clean and use either a virtual background that is original or personally branded. If you're doing a lot of video, considering using a program like Descript, which can give you a more personally branded look on video. While on camera, make sure your head is the focal point and you don't sit too far back which can make a person look small compared to everyone else.

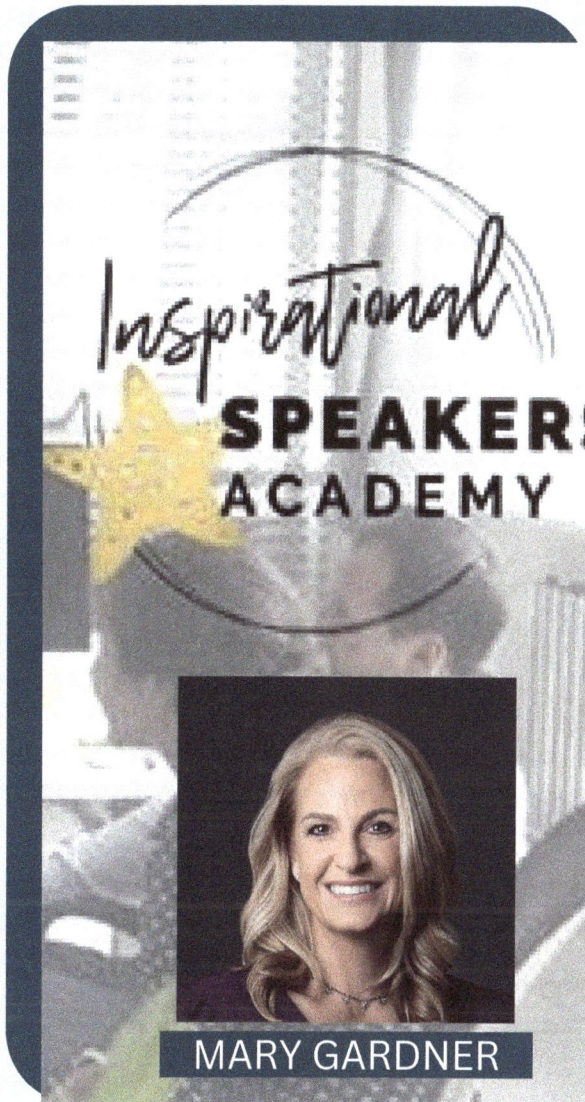

4. For the on-stage personality, a likeable and warm personality is always going to outshine someone who gets down to business quickly. Taking time to warm up a crowd with positive energy and small talk is a great way to establish credibility and gain fans. For extra support, I offer a workshop online: Introvert to Influencer: How to Connect, Communicate and Captivate; at https://marygardner.samcart.com/products/introvert

5. To excel on stage or video, having your message written is key. Short videos win the views! Start your presentation outlining a problem. Then share empathy for the listener, the cost if they don't change, and then present solution.

6. Practice your presentations before presenting. If you're bored, the audience will be bored. Rehearse using many tones of voices and different paces. This will keep you entertained and if you video yourself multiple times, you'll be able to see yourself improve before your very eyes!

7. Know and practice your personal stories. What did you learn from them and what is important for the audience to know about that story? For the longer version of speaking, it's important to know people will remember on average of just TWO stories and how they FELT around you!

MARY GARDNER

8. Tape all of your speeches! From the stage to the short messages you create. They can all be edited into smaller "sound bites" and put out on social media to draw people into your message and company.

9. Seek feedback. If you're committed to overcoming the fear and embracing the new world of thought leaders becoming branded "celebrities" then you're going to understand it takes about 100 days before you start looking and feeling like a pro. So give yourself some grace when you get suggestions on how to improve. Keep incorporating these suggestions in and things will continue to get better.

10. Practice! Practice! Practice! Don't forget, TV Anchors practice EVERY SINGLE DAY before going on the air. They read their script out loud, to perfect it. After a lot of practice, you'll be able to "wing it" and sound good. But take the time to speak a lot on camera and on stage in order to gain the experience you need to grow your confidence.

Becoming a public personality has a LOT of benefits. As a thought leader, you can control your message by writing it and delivering it in a multitude of platforms. Being likeable and authentic can go a long way to make the audience feel certain that you and your company will take care of them. They will be drawn to work with you and your company the more you deliver positive, inspiring, and informational messages that educate and entertain.

Taking a leap like this is taking a leap into the future.

You can do it! One step at a time!

Your stage is Waiting!

Mary Gardner is the CEO of Mary Gardner Communications and the Inspirational Speakers Academy. She has coached and trained thousands of speakers, thought leaders and influencers over the past 20 years. Her clients have made millions of dollars after her coaching and have transformed into some of the top inspiring speakers of our day, US Senators, Mayors, Public Figures, Successful authors, Paid TV spokespeople, and popular CEO's. She's appeared on hundreds of TV and Radio and Newspaper articles spots including ABC's 20/20, The Today Show, CNN, Good Morning America, CBS This AM, The Wall Street Journal, USA Today and a local show near you! She's a former publicist, Celebrity Lecture Agent, Wall Street Corporate Trainer, and owner of one of the first coach training companies in the world.

Mary can be reached at www.marygardner.com, where you will find free resources, connected with on LinkedIn at www.linkedin.com/marygardnercommunications and for a meeting: http://calendly.com/marygardner

Her two speaker bootcamps including a TEDx Bootcamp are online and available at www.marygardner.com

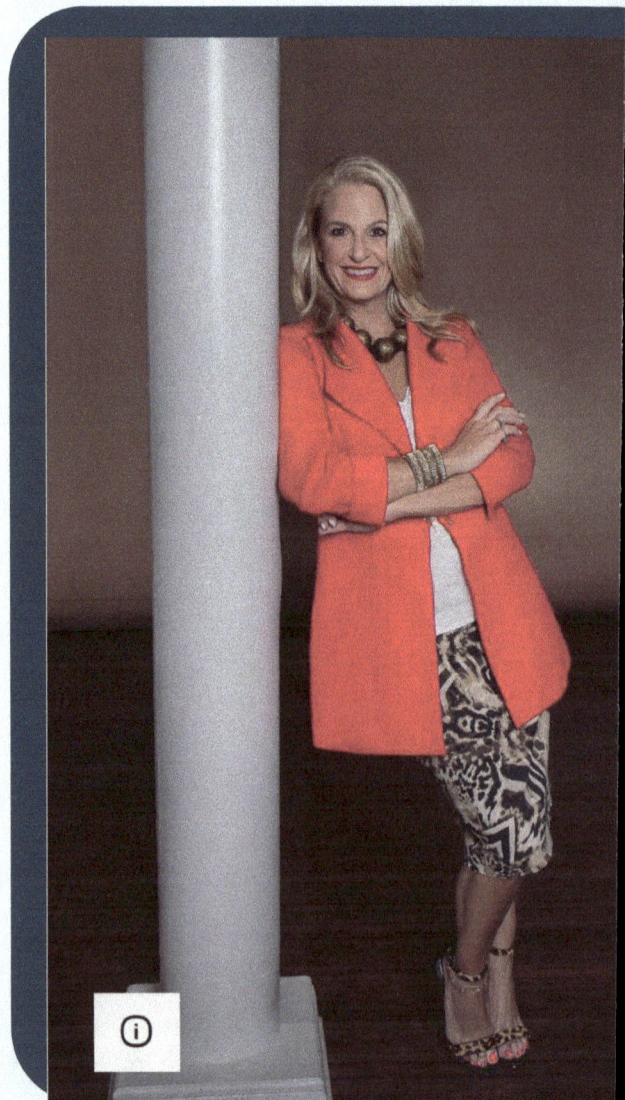

Photos By: Rinat Halon Photography

NYPPEX CEO Allen: Private Equity Funds to Seek Joint Ventures to Offset Slowdown in Exits

NEW YORK, Sept. 22, 2022 /PRNewswire/ -- NYPPEX Holdings, one of the world's leading providers of secondary private equity liquidity and data, today announced its projection that general partners in private equity funds will seek joint ventures for their older funds to offset the slowdown in exits.

"As the US Fed continues to raise interest rates and unrealized value in private equity funds remains historically high, expect a challenging exit environment in 2023," states Laurence Allen, CEO of NYPPEX.

For the first 6 months of 2022, NYPPEX estimates that for buyout funds worldwide, exit value from global IPOs declined over 70% year over year, while sponsor to sponsor/strategic transactions declined over 35%.

Given the current market environment, NYPPEX believes private investment holding periods may lengthen by 2 years or more for many private equity, venture and real estate funds worldwide.

"For general partners to continue to generate distributions to investors, particularly for their 2017 and earlier vintage private equity, venture and real estate funds, we believe SPV JVs will increasingly play an important role," stated Allen.

Benefits of a SPV JV for general partners may include the opportunity to immediately take out cash to make distributions and to participate in the upside of investments.

However, JV deal structures are typically available only to general partners that can contribute at least $50 million of private investments to the SPV.

● ● ● ● ● ● ● ● ● ● ● ● ● ● ● ● ● ● ●

About Laurence G. Allen

Laurence Allen serves as the CEO of NYPPEX Holdings, LLC. Since 1999, he has been a pioneer in the development of secondary markets in private equity funds and private companies.

He has been a speaker at numerous private equity conferences worldwide, including the Institutional Limited Partners Association Spring Conference (Miami), Super Return Middle East Conference (Abu Dhabi), Dow Jones Private Equity Outlook Conference (New York), World Exchange Congress Conference (Barcelona), Private Company Stock Conference (Palo Alto), and Asian Venture Capital & Private Equity Conference (Hong Kong).

Mr. Allen has served on numerous advisory boards including the Wharton School, Bowery Mission and the U.S. Congress Business Council. Prior to founding NYPPEX, Mr. Allen served in various positions with Merrill Lynch where he helped pioneer the development of secondary markets for commercial and residential mortgages. At Bear Stearns, he helped develop the secondary markets for private debt placements. Mr. Allen received a BS in Economics and MBA in Finance from the Wharton School at the University of Pennsylvania. https://laurenceallen.com/

ABOUT NYPPEX HOLDINGS

PPEX Holdings is one of the world's leading providers of secondary liquidity and data services for interests in alternative funds. Its clients include alternative investment funds, financial institutions, endowments, foundations, institutional investors, family offices, private clients and their respective advisors worldwide.

Since 2004, the NYPPEX QMS™ has been formerly recognized by the U.S. Internal Revenue Service as a Qualified Matching Service for private partnerships though a private letter ruling under internal Revenue Code §1.7704. The NYPPEX QMS assists private equity funds meet the requirements of a QMS safe-harbor exemption under IRS §1.7704, which helps ensure regulatory compliance and avoid an adverse taxable event when permitting higher volumes of secondary interest transfers annually. Its private securities are privately offered to qualified investors through NYPPEX, LLC. NYPPEX is regulated in the U.S. by the SEC and FINRA. Member FINRA, SPIC. https://nyppex.com/

It's Not Your Mother's Breast Cancer

For Breast Cancer Awareness Last Month, _"Rock Your Midlife"_ Radio Show Will Share Why

Ellen Albertson

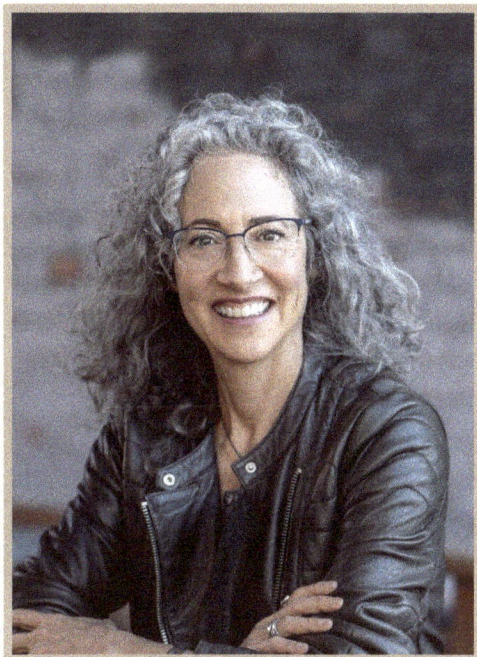

Program host Dr. Ellen, aka The Midlife Whisperer™, is a breast cancer survivor who shares lessons learned and progress made.

BURLINGTON, Vt., -Breast cancer survivor Ellen Albertson, a psychologist, registered dietician, and national board-certified health and wellness coach, will mark the 35th anniversary of the start of Breast Cancer Awareness Month by making the subject the focus throughout October on her weekly "Rock Your Midlife" radio program, available on Voice America. The show airs live from 2 p.m. to 3 p.m. Eastern on Wednesdays; available on all major podcast platforms, it reaches a global audience that includes the U.S., UK, China, Greece, Netherlands, Germany, Spain, Ukraine, Russia, Chile, Japan, New Zealand, and Spain.

Dr. Ellen, the author of Rock Your Midlife: 7 Steps to Transform Yourself and Make Your Next Chapter Your Best Chapter, now knows that a breast cancer diagnosis can happen to anyone — even someone like her who had no family history of the disease and was living a healthy lifestyle. Luckily, her diagnosis was made early (1A) and within 30 days of beginning treatment she was in remission without losing her hair. What Dr. Ellen did not know was that she carries a BRCA mutation and that in combination with dense breasts increased her risk for the disease.

She wants people to know that even as President Biden announced the Cancer Moonshot program, substantial progress has already been made on the treatment options and survival rates of breast cancer patients. She points out that the five-year survival rate for patients with early diagnosis is now 99% and the overall death rate has decreased by 1% per year from 2013 to 2018, the result of treatment advances and earlier detection through screening.

In an interview, she can talk about:
- Warning signs women may miss and the importance of early detection
- How to advocate for yourself and incorporate both complementary and conventional treatments
- Lifestyle changes to make
- The power of a positive mindset

Book Discovery App

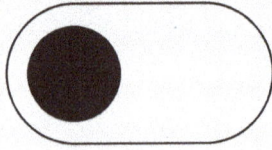

→ *to Mark Its Millionth Match as Users Swoon Over Book Dates*

WINTER PARK, Fla., Sept. 21, 2022 /PRNewswire/ -- When co-founders Brant Menswar and Jim Knight brainstormed a dating app to connect users to books rather than people, it seemed like an idea begging to become reality. Fast forward from that initial discussion in 2020 to tomorrow, as more than 50,000 registered users of Booky Call will celebrate the app's one-year anniversary and almost a million swipes..

Booky Call "ghostwrites" dating profiles for books. Users swipe right to set up a date with the book.

Booky Call is the fastest growing, free book discovery platform cleverly disguised as a dating app. It has found success by gamifying the process. "We took the psychology and functionality of dating apps to bring books to life," Menswar, the company's CEO, said. "Rather than browsing profiles and swiping right on Johns and Janes, our creative team 'ghostwrites' dating profiles for books so users can swipe right on their next 'book date'." The thousands of Johns and Janes in the "date-abase" range from classics to new releases, novels, and nonfiction titles from major publishing houses, indie publishers and self-published authors.

Given the proliferation of swiping, it's not surprising Booky Call has helped connect more than 50,000 active users to books across the globe. The company is counting down to its millionth swipe since launch, which it will celebrate at BookyCon, a virtual book festival in the Metaverse for book lovers and authors, set for Nov. 12.

Users scroll through a book's profile to learn details like its most attractive traits, what it spends time thinking about and its plans for their first date before deciding to swipe left or right. A right swipe leads to the book sending a DM with links to date it: asking to "meet in person" for the print version, "keep it digital" for the ebook or "whisper in your ear" for the audiobook. Users can then purchase the title in the chosen format from Bookshop, Libro.fm or Amazon.

Twice a week, the app sends users "you up?" messages with specially curated recommendations for those needing a "book up" rather than a hook up. Menswar admits the app leans in to the lighthearted innuendo. "Look," he said, "books don't scam you, stalk you or ghost you."

Valerie Willis, COO of 4 Horsemen Publishing, is excited to have several titles getting dates through the app. "The authors and readers seem to love this interaction," she said. Madison Taylor of Page Two, a Canadian-based publisher, agreed. "The profiles are so creative," she said.

Briah Krueger, who writes under the name of B.A. McRae, said she was impressed with the profiles, including the one for her debut. "Each book comes with details beyond your wildest bookish dreams, certainly more juicy deets than any synopsis or review," she wrote on her blog.

Booky Call is available for iOS and Android users.

MAKE IT HAPPEN

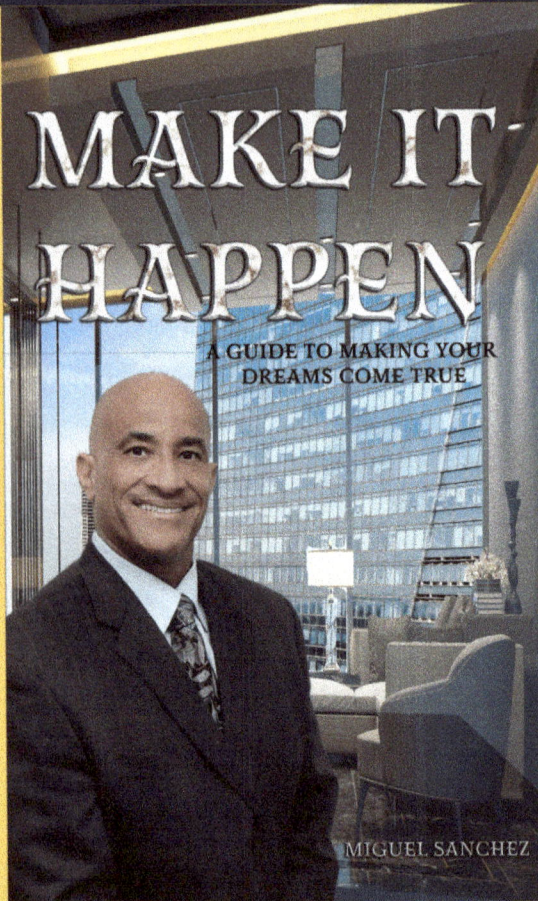

MAKE IT HAPPEN

A GUIDE TO MAKING YOUR DREAMS COME TRUE

MIGUEL SANCHEZ

A guide to making your dreams come true

MIGUEL SANCHEZ

FUNDING RESOURCES FOR ENTREPRENEURS

1. Angel Investors

If your business is a start-up, you may have access to a few different funding options. The first is an angel investor, who is a person interested in investing in a company as an entrepreneur. Angel investors can provide a one-time investment to help get the business off the ground or offer continuous support as the needs of the business grow and change. The difference between an angel investor and another type of investor is the focus on the success of the business, rather than reaping a big profit.

If you're interested in this option, try using online resources like AngelList or Gust to find potential investors. These websites focus on connecting small business owners with angel investors. Gust functions like a social network, allowing you to build relationships· and interact with investors. AngelList is more complicated, but you can set up a profile with an activity feed, which investors can view. All start-ups and potential investors registered on these sites have gone through a vetting process to make sure they're legitimate.

Angel.co

Gust.com

Angelinvestmentnetwork.co.uk

Angelcapitalassociation.org

Funded.com

Angelforum.org

Envestors.co.uk

Goldenseeds.com (for women only)

FUNDING RESOURCES FOR ENTREPRENEURS

Alta Partners

Sequoia Capital

Founder's Fund

Lightspeed Venture Partners

Susa Ventures

Atomico

Emergence Capital

First Round

FactoryMade

2. Venture Capital

The most common investment option for small businesses is venture capital. Venture capitalists will typically invest in companies with the potential for long-term growth. On the investor's side, the risk is high, because the growth is generally based on perception and projections. Investors continue to offer venture capital because of the potential for higher-than-average returns. For start-up companies with limited history, obtaining traditional funding is more challenging, so venture capital is a funding option that is within easier reach.

THE OTHER SIDE OF Privileged

…od story is
…Queen. On her
…mily takes her
… she meets her
… fateful day,
…e changes
… lady she meets
…trafficker who
…her family. Zoey
…J-working slave
…all opens up an
…nce, the attractive
…work with her, is
…e family's story.
…t him enough to
…her heart?
…of hope she's been
…ting for?

SHERI CHAPMAN

SHERI CHAPMAN

THE OTHER SIDE OF
Privileged

Trient Press

CHRISTMAS WREATHS

Ingredients

- 2 tablespoons butter
- Green food coloring
- 3 cups cornflakes
- Red M&M's minis (about 2 tablespoons)

Chocolate Sauce ingredients

- 300 ml liquid milk
- 60 gr sugar
- 25 cocoa powder
- 1/2 tsp cornstarch
- 100 gr dark cooking chocolate
- 1 egg yolk beaten off

Directions

- Place marshmallows and butter in a microwave-safe bowl; microwave, uncovered, on high until butter is melted and marshmallows are puffed, about 45 seconds. Tint with green food coloring. Stir in cornflakes.

- On a waxed paper-lined baking sheet, divide mixture into 8 portions. With buttered hands, working quickly, shape each portion into a 3-in. wreath. Decorate immediately with M&M's, pressing to adhere. Let stand until set.

Nutrition Facts

1 wreath: 134 calories, 4g fat (2g saturated fat), 9mg cholesterol, 116mg sodium, 25g carbohydrate (13g sugars, 0 fiber), 1g protein.

Sweet Potato Casserole
WITH CRUNCHY PECAN TOPPING

INGREDIENTS

8 SERVINGS

CASSEROLE
- 3 15 ounce cans of sweet potatoes. drained.

(The same amount of fresh sweet potatoes can be used, just peel and boil them until a fork can be inserted easily.)
- 1/4 cup melted butter
- 1/2 cup sugar
- 1/2 teaspoon salt
- 2 medium eggs well beaten
- 1/2 cup milk (or half and half to make it richer)
- 1/2 teaspoon vanilla

TOPPING
- 1 cup packed light-brown sugar
- 1/4 cup butter softened
- 1/3 cup flour
- 2 teaspoon cinnamon or season to taste
- 1.5 cups chopped pecans honey roasted or regular

DIRECTIONS

- Pour the butter over the sweet potatoes in a large bowl and mash.
- Add next 5 ingredients; sugar, salt, eggs, milk, and vanilla. blend well
- Pour into 9 in. glass baking dish
- Combine ingredients for topping and crumble with your hands until combined.
- Sprinkle the topping mixture over the potatoes.
- Bake @ 350 degrees for 40 minutes
- This can be made ahead! enjoy!

This can be made ahead, just make the casserole according to instructions, without baking. Cover it with aluminum foil and store in the refrigerator. When ready to serve, bake the casserole for 40-45 minutes at 350°F.

Traveling with Trient

THE AI4 CONVENTION:
A must-attend event for any technology-minded CEOs

Keeping up with today's changing market to better serve your business.

By: M.L. Ruscsak

This year Ai4 was held at the wonderful and exciting MGM Grand in Las Vegas, Nevada. Attendees coming together from across the globe not only to network but also educate on all that Ai has to offer.

So, what is Ai4? Ai4, short for artificial intelligence and machine learning, is one of the most important topics in technology today. In recent years, artificial intelligence and machine learning have proven to be essential technologies for businesses in virtually every industry, with AI being especially crucial for the cyber security industry. Despite its importance; however, AI is also one of the most controversial technologies out there, with many people worrying about the ethical ramifications of its rapid growth. Which is why an Ai4 convention should be on the calendar of every CEO who wants to take the next step forward in his or her company's digital transformation. We fear what we don't understand, yet we can't understand unless we attend events such as Ai4.

> **So let's dive in and cover reasons why you need to attend the next convention.**

What is Artificial Intelligence?

Artificial intelligence (AI) is the ability of a computer program or system to learn and solve problems. It has been around for centuries, but only recently has it become more advanced and widespread. AI is used in many different fields, such as medicine, finance, manufacturing, and even education. With so many different applications, it is no wonder that AI is one of the most talked-about topics in the business world today. If you are a CEO who is interested in staying ahead of the curve, then the Ai4 convention is a must-attend event. At this event, attendees will be able to network with other executives, get an overview of what's possible with machine learning, and talk about how AI can best be applied to their companies. In addition, the Ai4 2022 team will also be present at the event.

The main goal? To provide your company with an expert consultation on how they can leverage AI technologies in order to stay competitive in their industry. After all, artificial intelligence is one of the fastest growing sectors in the economy, and being unprepared means leaving money on the table. Attendees can expect to gain insight into data science methods and techniques during the conference sessions, while having opportunities to meet experts from prestigious institutions like MIT and Harvard. Once you have met with our consultants, we hope that your takeaway will be clear: AI should not just be something that businesses consider; it should be a core part of their growth strategy.

Where was Ai4 held?

Before we get into too much detail about the conference itself, we must first go into the location, so we get a full understanding of Ai4. This convection was held at the wonderful MGM Grand hotel, in Las Vegas, Nevada. As Las Vegas is a hub of conventions having the full gambit of hotels, restaurants, convention space and of course places for entertainment. It only makes sense when spending days at one location to make sure the guest don't need to stray too far form the reason they are attending. In that event the MGM grand made the event outstanding to attend just by doing some little things. From online hotel booking, keeping the guest in the same room blocks and having outstanding meals for lunch.

Don't let the convention fool you we still had plenty of time to play and explore all that MGM offers.

> *Despite its importance, AI is also one of the most controversial technologies out there.*

Ai4 the Global Connection

The Ai4 convention is a three-day event that brings together business leaders and data practitioners to facilitate the responsible adoption of artificial intelligence and machine learning across multiple sectors. This is a much-needed event for any CEO who is technology minded. The convention will provide an opportunity to learn from some of the best minds in the industry, make global connections, and get a better understanding of how AI can be used responsibly to benefit businesses and society as a whole. Global connection and leadership will be explored through thought provoking panels, engaging speakers, live demos with attendees collaborating on topics related to their areas of expertise and experience. Attendees are encouraged to participate actively in sessions which promise to empower attendees with new perspectives on how technology can help them innovate more responsibly or lead differently than ever before. Global Connection and Leadership will be explored through thought provoking panels, engaging speakers, live demos with attendees collaborating on topics related to their areas of expertise and experience. Technology in today's world is all encompassing and finding opportunities to create global connections while at the same time making technology accessible to everyone – no matter what region they come from -should continue at this pace going forward.

Why Attend Ai4?

If you're a CEO who is looking to adopt artificial intelligence and machine learning in your business, then the Ai4 convention is a must-attend event. Held over three days, the Ai4 convention brings together business leaders and data practitioners to facilitate the responsible adoption of AI and ML across multiple sectors. This is an invaluable opportunity to network with other like-minded individuals and learn from some of the best in the field. The conference has expert speakers, panels, and workshops to provide essential insights into how AI can be used for different purposes such as fraud detection or marketing. For example, one speaker explained how his company was able to predict 80% of their customers' purchases based on their past purchasing habits and data analysis (lessons learned). Other speakers discuss the ethics behind using AI software without permission or about how it might affect hiring practices in the future.

Where it will take us in the future?

As with any industry Ai is quickly becoming the number one key part in any business. From healthcare to security and everything in-between. The current Ai is only limited to the minds of those who create it. However, with every new line of code created there will tend to be a decline in today's job market while those with the abilities to program or analyze the data become more in demand. In closing, we are going to see an increase in this gap between the haves and have nots as machines continue their rise in society.

Ai4 provides access to some of these developing technologies as well as more advanced Ai systems like quantum computers, blockchain platforms, wearable tech, genetic engineering, and biotechnology. All leading into what promises to be an even more innovative future than before.

> *The current AI is only limited to the minds of those who create it.*

5 REASONS TO PLAN YOUR NEXT VACATION TO THE MGM GRAND IN LAS VEGAS

If you're looking to get away to Las Vegas and want to experience something different, look no further than the MGM Grand. This legendary hotel and casino has everything you need in order to have the time of your life. Check out these five reasons why you should vacation at this top-notch resort on your next trip.

1.) Spectacular Hospitality

The MGM Grand Hotel and Casino is a unique resort offering an unforgettable experience for visitors. The hotel features a world-class casino, the Level Up sports lounge, a grand pool complex featuring three pools, lazy rivers and whirlpools, with top-notch amenities which include signature treatments from the iconic Grand Spa.

2.) Energetic Atmosphere

With so many options for activities it's hard to pick just one. Visitors looking for luxury will be pleased with what they find at the MGM Grand Hotel and Casino as every detail has been carefully considered making this a truly magnificent experience. For example, when you book your stay, you are offered a welcome amenity that changes nightly from fresh fruit and nuts to sweets from the room service menu. Guests also receive complimentary breakfast buffet vouchers for two daily that can be used at either of their two onsite restaurants or via room service delivery.

When staying here we highly recommend trying out the in-room dining menu which offers healthy eating plans like gluten free menus or low-calorie selections along with plenty of flavorful dishes like steak frites with roasted vegetables or black cod albacore ceviche.

The hotel also offers top notch amenities such as golfing, fitness center and pools; there really is no end to what guests can do while visiting this incredible destination.

3.) Luxurious Rooms

The rooms at the MGM are designed with your comfort and relaxation in mind. The spacious suites have a level of sophistication that is unmatched by any other hotel on the strip. With plush, king-sized beds, marble bathrooms, and plenty of amenities, you'll be sure to enjoy every second of your stay.

You can't go wrong with any option when staying at MGM so make your reservations today!

4.) Great Restaurants

MGM offers restaurant selections featuring celebrity chefs such as:

- Chef Masaharu Morimoto -Morimoto of Las Vegas, which features exciting Japanese-American cuisine.
- Chef Joël Robuchon- Restaurant Joël Robuchon featuring an unparalleled French menu.
- Chef Wolfgang Puck- Wolfgang Puck Bar & Grill that showcases his talents and features some of his most popular comfort foods.

Restaurants at MGM Grand vary from Italian, BBQ, Steakhouses, Creole, and American, to Pan-Asian, French, Japanese, Chinese, and Mediterranean. Whatever your taste buds desire, there's fabulous foods that will satisfy.

1. Other popular restaurants include Nellie's Southern Kitchen, Hakkasan - Las Vegas. Emeril's New Orleans Fish House, Gallagher's Steakhouse, Crush - MGM Grand 7. Morimoto - MGM Grand, Craftsteak - MGM Grand, and Hard Rock Cafe - Las Vegas - The Strip. You can also grab some great drinks at BetMGM Bar or Level Up - America's first sports lounge bar.

The restaurants on property have been revamped and offer a great selection of food, from fast casual to fine dining. For a quick bite head over to Nathan's Famous Hotdogs then pick up some Häagen-Dazs. We would be remiss if we failed to encourage you not to miss the Grand Buffet at the MGM Grand which offers one of the largest selections of menu items for the Breakfast, Weekend Brunch, and Dinner Buffets.

MGM partners with many travel companies, so check with them to see if comped buffet passes are available to you.

5.) Exciting Nightlife

With over 100,000 square feet of casino space, there's never a dull moment. And if you find yourself feeling adventurous, you can try your luck on one of our many slot machines or gaming tables. Ready for more? Head up to the world-famous poker room where you can compete against some of the best players in town and test your skills at Texas Hold'em or Omaha. And that's just the beginning.

When it comes to fun after dark, the MGM has everything from tantalizing nightclubs like Hakkasan Nightclub to sophisticated cocktail lounges like 32°, not to mention everything else in between. If variety is what you're looking for, you'll find it all at the MGM Grand.

Need a new outfit before heading out on the town? A relaxing treatment at the spa? Or perhaps something tasty from our in-room dining menu? Whatever you're looking for, it's yours when you stay with MGM.

BY: ML USCSAK
EXPLORE THE WORLD

Otherworld

**An Interactive Museum
Blurring the Line Between
Fiction and Reality**

Booking Now

614.868.3631

Otherworld | Immersive Art
Experience (otherworldohio.com)

WHAT IS OTHERWORLD?

Otherworld is where imagination meets innovation. The interactive museum is for all ages as it has many different exhibits.

- Otherworld is a 32,000 square foot facility that is filled with large-scale works of art.

- There are secret passages and playgrounds that blur the line between reality, science fiction, and fantasy.

- Otherworld is an interactive museum where you can see art or enjoy family fun.

- There is artwork made by more than 40 artists in the showroom.

- Guests can also walk through rooms that are anything from science lab to den of spiders.

- Family fun includes crawling through spaces to find a beanbag lounge to rest and socialize.

What Makes it Unique?

More than 40 artists have collaborated to transform this facility into an immersive art installation. Visitors can walk through otherworldly landscapes, explore hidden passages, and play in fantastical spaces that blur the line between fiction and reality. The exhibition includes large-scale paintings, video installations, sound pieces, sculptures, and interactive games. The artists are from 16 countries and they are each using different mediums such as sculpture or painting to express their visions of what it means to be human.

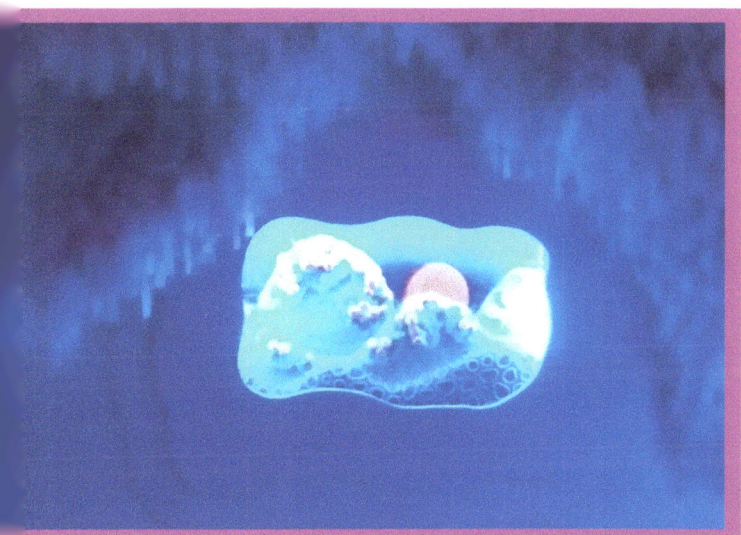

Should You Visit?

Our vote is ABSOLUTELY. If you're looking for a museum with an interactive twist and something off the beaten path, there's a new place in town.

This incredible art installation is located at 5819 Chantry Drive, Columbus, Ohio 43232.

For reservation & information call: 614.868.3631
www.otherworldohio.com

T R I E N T   N E W S

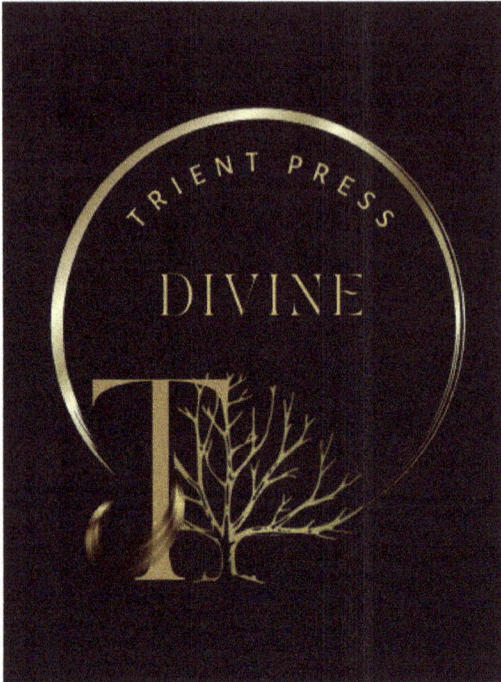

Get ready for more great reads from Trient Press! We're expanding our reach to bring you even more voices from around the world. Over the past few months Trient has been reaching out to expand outreach and enrich the minds of our readers by adding new voices and stories. In doing so, Trient Press has added a special new imprint called Trient Divine. Our sole purpose with adding this imprint is to bring you uplifting and motivational stories from industry leaders, community activist, as well as others who want to share their powerful words and testimonies with the world.

The voices of Trient Press are always evolving, adding new genres in the fictional arena as well as adding to our non-fictional collection; however, we are not done there!

We are excited to announce that we have finally syndicated Dove and Dragon Radio on our wonderful sister stations both nationally and globally. We are launching the new website, www.doveanddragonradio.com so that we are better able to reach our listeners and audiences from around the globe.

Looking to tell your story? Just look for the booking information on the Dove and Dragon website.

All of our book imprints can be found at www. Trientpress.com.

As always, stay current with all that Trient has going on at www.trientmagazine.com.

After all, 1.1 million subscribers can't be wrong.

TRIENT SNIPPETS

Arshisa Adejiyan

As A well-rounded leader, speaker, recording artist and life coach. We had the opportunity to sit down with Arshia during a dove and dragon interview to find out more about what she does at her company Spontaneous Queen.

Getting into shapeware and body countering she is adding ways to benefit those in today's society in order to bring out their natural beauty both inside and out.
Keep up with Arshisa at
SpontaneousQueen.Com

enea Linsom

Recently we at Trient Press were ble to speak to Renae about her Company Greatness Inc.
ike so many great writers out there 's refreshing not to just speak to an uthor about a solo project but a vriter who is there to help guide uthors to their next big project.
Vith Greatness Inc, the ability to vrite blogs, short articles and yes hostwrite novels has never been asier.

www.ingramcontent.com/pod-product-compliance
Lightning Source LLC
Chambersburg PA
CBHW041225220326
41597CB00038BA/6323